WONDERS OF OUR WORLD

Carron Brown

Illustrated by Stef Murphy

Kane Miller
A DIVISION OF EDC PUBLISHING

Journey across our world to see
Earth's incredible wonders.
Peer inside ancient buildings, climb
mighty mountains, dive under the
surface of the sea, and much more.

Shine a flashlight behind the page or
hold the book up to the light to reveal
what is hidden in and around each wonder.
Discover a world of great surprises!

In Arizona, the Colorado River winds its way through the Grand Canyon. This is one of the world's deepest canyons.

People ride in rafts down the river. Can you see anyone else?

There are people riding mules
along a tunnel inside the rock.

The canyon is about one mile deep.
A trip to the bottom and back
can take two days!

In 1943, something strange happened
in a field in Mexico. A farmer saw smoke
coming out of a crack in the ground.

what happened to the crack?

It became the Paricutín volcano!

The volcano grew up and up. It is now
9,186 feet high. That's as high as a
1,000-story building would be!

These people have climbed up a mountain in Peru to visit the ancient city of Machu Picchu.

What did the city look like when it was first built?

The Inca people built the
city about 550 years ago.

After only 100 years, it was
abandoned, but no one knows why.

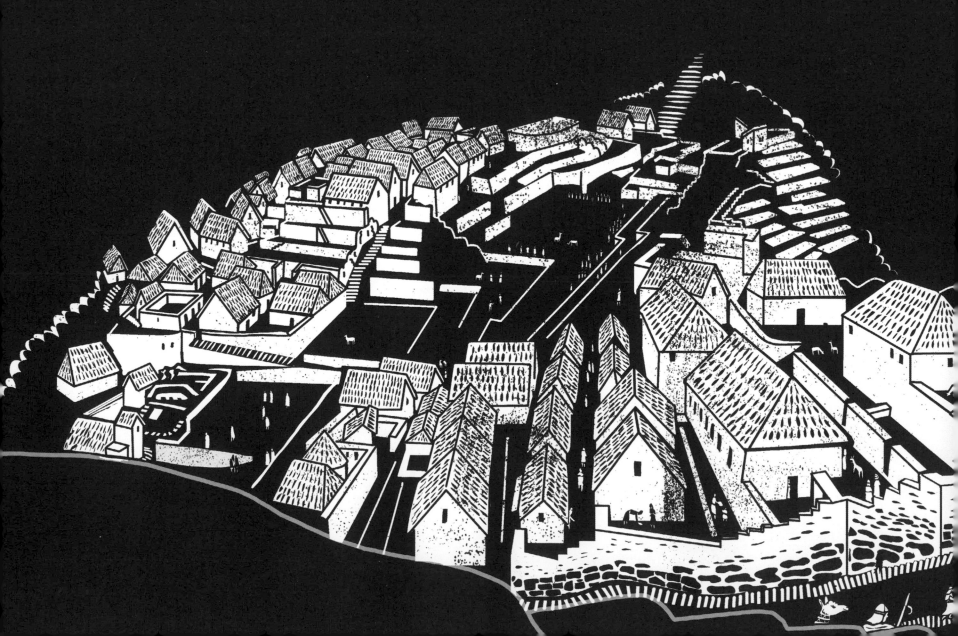

These people
are walking
between two
walls of rock
in Jordan.

What is in
front of them?

It's a temple carved into the rock!

The building is part of an ancient city called
Petra. It is more than 2,000 years old.

There's a huge, sprawling wonder
of the world in Cape Town, South Africa.
It's famous for being covered with
blankets of white cloud.

What is it?

It's one of the world's oldest mountains. It is called Table Mountain because it has a flat top like a table.

People say that the cloud looks like a fluffy tablecloth.

The Christ the
Redeemer statue
stands high on
a mountain
in Brazil.

What's below the cloud?

It's the huge city
of Rio de Janeiro.

The statue is so tall
that it can be seen from
every area of the city.

These animals are in the rain forest in Southern Africa.

Where is this mist coming from?

It's Victoria Falls—the world's biggest waterfall!

The mist above it is known as "The Smoke That Thunders" because the sound of the river is so loud.

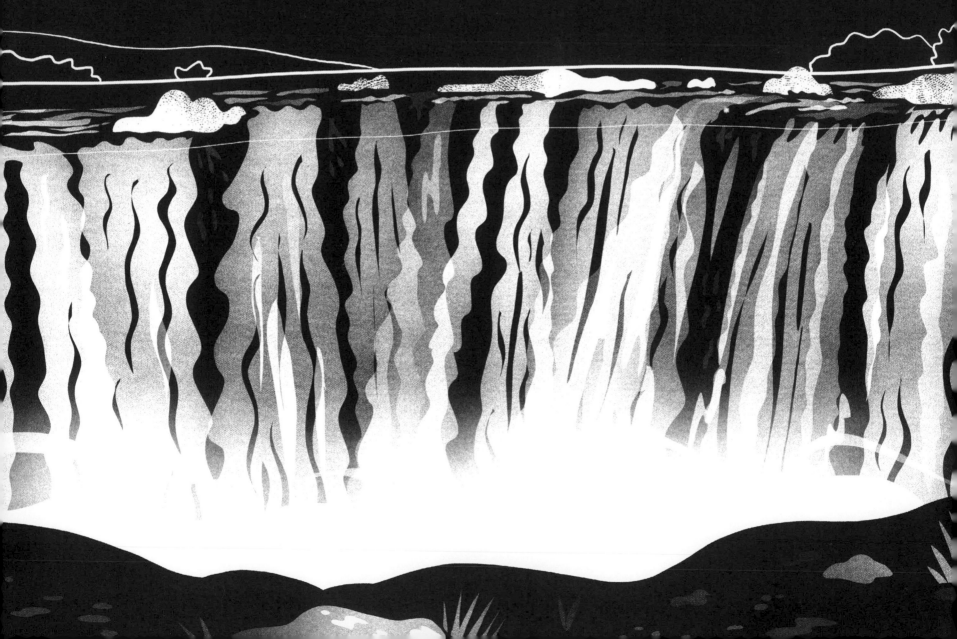

This ruined building in Rome, Italy,
is visited by many people every day.

What was it used for long ago?

The Colosseum was an enormous,
round, open-air stadium built
by the Romans about
2,000 years ago.

Audiences of up to 50,000 came here to
watch warriors, called gladiators, fight.

This beautiful building is in India. It's called the Taj Mahal and it took 22 years to build.

What was it built for?

It may look like a palace, but it's really a
memorial, built by an emperor for his wife.

Main dome

Central chamber

Minaret

Underground tombs

The tombs of the emperor and his
wife are in a crypt below the ground.

The Himalayas are a group of mountains in Asia. One of these mountains is the tallest in the world—Mount Everest.

Who do you think is inside these tents?

Climbers are resting in these tents after a day's climb. It takes many days to reach the top and the temperature never gets above freezing.

The Great Wall of China is an ancient
wall that stretches for thousands of miles.

It still
stands today,
but what was
it built for?

It was built to keep out invaders!

Soldiers in towers along the wall watched for trouble.

These hot-air balloons are floating across the sky of Bagan, in Myanmar.

What are the passengers looking at?

They have come to see the ancient
temples. There are more than
2,000 temples in Bagan.

People built them about
a thousand years ago.

These strange-looking islands
are in Ha Long Bay, Vietnam.

There are up to 2,000 of them.
How do tourists visit them?

They travel on boats, which wind in and out of small inlets between the islands.

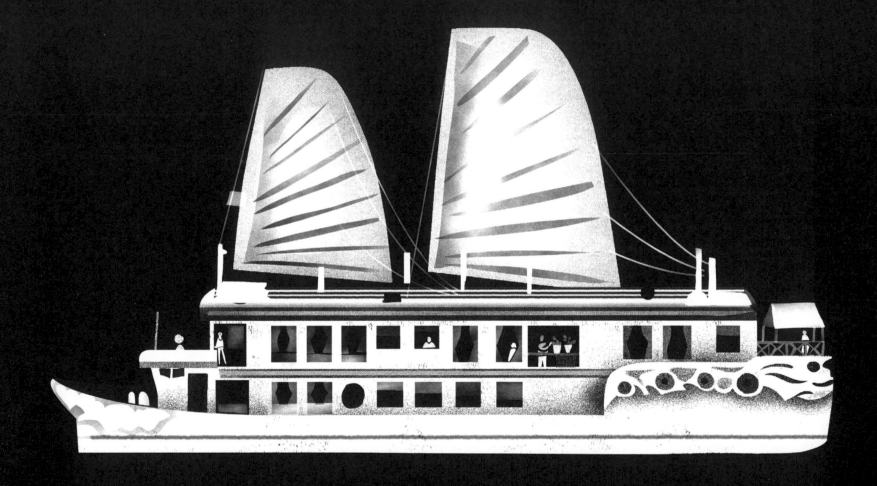

This boat tour in the Philippines is heading toward a cave.

Why are people wearing hard hats?

There are long spikes of rock called
stalactites dangling from the ceiling.

The boat will travel through the
cave on an underground river
called the Puerto Princesa.

The Great Barrier Reef in Australia is the world's largest coral reef. It is made of tiny living creatures called corals.

What else lives in the reef?

Lots and lots of reef fish hide among the corals.

Some smell like the coral and others look like the coral so that predators cannot find them.

Many wonders of our world were made by people long ago. Others were formed by nature and more continue to be made today.

The world is full of small wonders too—remember to watch out for them!

There's more...

Scale mountains, hide in coral and spy from the sky to find out more about the man-made marvels, ancient peoples and natural wonders of our world.

Temple A temple is a building that people visit to worship and pray. Temples tend to be magnificent and fill worshippers with awe. The impressive Angkor Wat in Cambodia is the largest Hindu temple in the world.

Mountain Mountains are the highest places on Earth. They cover about a quarter of our world. There are even lots of mountains underwater in the ocean! Maunakea in Hawai'i is taller than Mount Everest if measured from its base under the sea.

Reef The Great Barrier Reef in Australia is the largest living structure on Earth! About 1,500 species of fish live here. But reefs like this one are sensitive. Hot temperatures or too much sunlight can bleach and kill the corals—leaving no food or homes for the fish.

Statue A statue is the likeness of a person or an animal that is made using a solid material, such as stone, wood or metal. Humans have made statues for centuries. Some statues from Ancient Greece survive today and tell the tales of their long-gone makers.

Volcano A volcano is a mountain with a hole at the top called a crater. Red-hot, runny lava and ash burst out through the crater when the volcano erupts. The ancient Roman city of Pompeii in Italy was buried after a volcanic eruption. Today the site is visited by millions of tourists.

Inca The Inca people lived about 600 years ago in South America. As many as 12 million Inca lived around the Andes mountains. They adapted to living at high altitudes and are thought to have had larger lungs and slower hearts than other humans.

The Romans The Romans lived 2,000 years ago across Europe, North Africa and Asia. The capital of the Roman world was Rome, in Italy. They invented and developed many things, including our calendar!

First American Edition 2018
Kane Miller, A Division of EDC Publishing

Copyright © 2018 Quarto Publishing plc

For information contact:
Kane Miller, A Division of EDC Publishing
PO Box 470663
Tulsa, OK 74147-0663
www.kanemiller.com
www.edcpub.com
www.usbornebooksandmore.com

Library of Congress Control Number: 2017958223

Printed in China

ISBN: 978-1-61067-718-9

2 3 4 5 6 7 8 9 10